# SIR TOM FINNEY

*A life in pictures*

**Lancashire Evening Post**

# SIR TOM FINNEY

## *A life in pictures*

FOREWORD BY
SIR BOBBY CHARLTON

# Acknowledgements

With thanks to Lancashire Evening Post photographers past and present and the National Football Museum.

First published in Great Britain in 2009 by
The Breedon Books Publishing Company Limited
Breedon House, 3 The Parker Centre,
Derby, DE21 4SZ.

This paperback edition published in Great Britain in 2013 by
DB Publishing, an imprint of JMD Media Ltd

ISBN 978-1-78091-384-1

Printed and bound in the UK by Copytech (UK) Ltd Peterborough

# Contents

Sir Tom aged 13

Sir Tom aged 83

# A Message

Legend is a word that, these days, seems to be overused.

Often it crops up when describing this football player or that but many, if the truth be told, do not merit such a tag.

But that is certainly not the case for Sir Tom Finney. He is exactly that – a genuine football legend - and one of the greatest players this country has ever produced.

Sir Tom played for Preston North End in a bygone era in the 1940s and 1950s, appearing 433 times and scoring 187 goals.

As a child Finney lived a stone's throw away from Preston's ground at Deepdale and by the time he was 14 the club had discovered his talents and offered him a contract. But his father made him complete his apprenticeship in the family plumbing business before he signed as a professional.

The Second World War, where Sir Tom served in Italy and Egypt, meant that he did not make his League debut for the club until 1946. A tricky player with an eye-for-goal, who could play on the flank or up front, Finney immediately became a favourite with the Preston faithful.

That same year he made his debut for England. He won 76 caps and scored 30 goals for his country – a notable highlight when he scored twice against the then reigning World Champions Italy in Turin in 1948, as England won 4-0.

Sadly Sir Tom's outstanding form for club and country for the best part of two decades did not result in any major honours, bar a Second Division championship for Preston. The personal accolades came though – he was Footballer of the Year in 1953-54 and again in 1956-57 - but Preston North End fell just short of silverware, coming second to Arsenal in the First Division in 1953 and losing the 1954 FA Cup Final to West Brom.

Yet Sir Tom will always be seen as one of English football's finest. His conduct on the pitch was exemplary just as it was off it – he was never ever booked, let alone sent off.

Following his retirement as a player in 1960, Preston's favourite son continued to give back to the community with tireless work for charity, as well as becoming chairman of the local health authority.

Knighted in 1998, he remains president of Preston North End and the National Football Museum.

I hope all who pick this book up enjoy this special tribute to the man. After all, there is only one Sir Tom Finney.

**GERRY SUTCLIFFE MP, MINISTER FOR SPORT**

# Foreword

During my career I was privileged to play alongside some great footballers, and Sir Tom Finney was right up there with the very best of them.

When I made my debut for England I was 19 years old and I was in awe of him. We were introduced to the Duke of Gloucester and there next to me was my hero. We were playing against Scotland in a British Home Championship match at Hampden Park in front of 127,000 fans. I scored the third goal with a volley and we went on to win the game 4-0, but Tom had left his own mark on the day for me. People talked about my goal being unstoppable but that was all thanks to the super cross Tom Finney provided from the left wing to set it up. I can still hear the sound of the ball lashing against the net and after that, all you could hear was the silence. I think Tom enjoyed it even more because his great pal and teammate at Preston North End Tommy Docherty was the Scottish captain that day. I know he is very proud that he never lost a game at Hampden Park.

I remember another time watching Tom take a corner for England and Stan Mortensen scored and ran across to thank him. In another game Mortensen scored from a Stanley Matthews corner and he again thanked him. But in another game Mortensen scored from a Bobby Langton corner and said nothing. Later I asked him why. 'Because Finney and Matthews always made sure the laces were facing away from my head,' he replied.

His team mates certainly loved him and for a wide player his goalscoring record was phenomenal. Thirty goals in 76 games for England and half a century later he is still among the leading goalscorers for his country. If it had not been for the war then his England records would undoubtedly have been even higher.

The fact he won his first cap just one month after making his debut for Preston North End gives you an idea just how good a footballer he was.

We only played together for England five times and there were some great players around in those days, the likes of Johnny Haynes, Nat Lofthouse and our captain Billy Wright, but everyone respected Tom for his wonderful ability. He was one of the world's top players, without question.

His last game for England was at Wembley against USSR. We won a penalty and Tom, who usually took the penalties, handed the ball to me and I scored. We won the game 5-0, but it is a gesture I have never forgotten, especially as it turned out to be the final time he wore the England shirt he was always so proud to pull on.

It was typical of Tom. He is a wonderful person and I am proud to consider him a good personal friend. Away from football his unmatched contribution to life in his beloved Preston since retirement is a measure of the man and it is no surprise he is as loved and revered now as he was in his playing days.

**SIR BOBBY CHARLTON**

*'I lived in Holme Slack which was a stone's throw from Deepdale and, of course, as a youngster I always wanted to play for my home-town team.'*

Sir Tom Finney

# CHAPTER ONE
# *Family*

*'As a man I found him an exceptional person with great values and a great feeling for Preston North End. It was a privilege to sit down in his company and talk about the game.'*
Former Preston North End manager David Moyes

A family snapshot from 1928 with Aunt Florrie, great-grandfather Riley, grandma Mitchell, cousin Billy Shufflebottom, Sir Tom and brother Joe.

The Deepdale Modern School Dawson Cup Final winners in 1936. The team beat St Ignatious 1–0, and Sir Tom (pictured fourth from the left, front row) was the goalscorer.

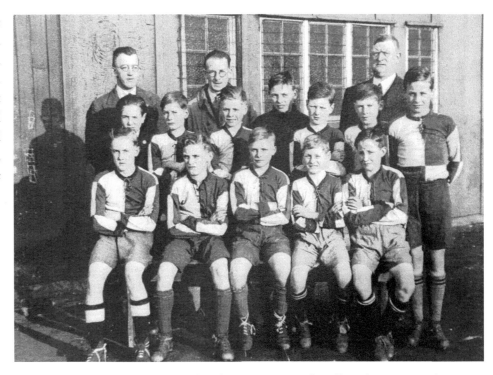

Sir Tom enjoys a break during war service in Venice with Glasgow Rangers' Willie Thornton and George Hamilton of Aberdeen.

Sir Tom married Lady Elsie on 1 November 1945 in Emmanuel Church, Preston, after being granted special leave from serving with the armed forces in Italy. The pair met in St Jude's Dancehall when Elsie, who always loved dancing, was just 18. They began courting when she was 19 and got engaged when Tom joined the wartime forces in 1942.

'Elsie and I got married in the local church and had our reception at St Jude's Hall in Preston, the place we'd met at a Saturday night dance a few years before. There was nothing in the papers because nobody really knew who we were then. I didn't make my England debut until September 1946 and Elsie worked at a Preston steam laundry. I only earned 12s/10d a week as a footballer back then and I don't remember how much our wedding cost. It was definitely peanuts. But the most important thing was for Elsie and I to be married.'

Sir Tom Finney

An intimate set of photographs of Sir Tom, Lady Elsie and their children, Barbara and Brian, taken by the *Lancashire Evening Post* at the family home ahead of the 1954 FA Cup Final.

Sir Tom with his daughter Barbara.

Sir Tom with Lady Elsie, Barbara (8) and Brian (10) on his 36th birthday.

Fellow Preston North End player Tommy Docherty and Sir Tom Finney's families enjoy a day out together.

Brian Finney tries on one of Sir Tom's England caps for size.

Sir Tom puts son Brian through his paces on the Deepdale pitch.

Sir Tom combined his job as a plumber with his role at Preston North End.

'*After the trial with Preston North End I must have done reasonably well because they approached my father about me becoming a professional footballer, or what they were known as in those days, the ground staff. Much to my surprise my father said he's not prepared to do that, he will play on a part-time basis and do his training during the day because I have got him a job as a plumber, as an apprentice, which was difficult to get in those days, and he said you must serve your time as a plumber and you will always have something to fall back on.*'

Sir Tom Finney

Sir Tom stands proudly outside his business premises in Preston...
... and bringing his trade to Deepdale during the building of the new Deepdale Stadium.

Sir Tom and Lady Elsie enjoy a night out and are pictured below at home together.

Sir Tom addresses councillors to thank them for awarding him the Freedom of Preston.

Sir Tom and Lady Elsie celebrate his being awarded the Freedom of Preston.

Sir Tom Finney kisses his wife Elsie after walking across the red carpet on the Deepdale pitch before the Preston North End v Stockport County FA Cup third-round match in January 1998.

Sir Tom gets kitted out for his day at Buckingham Palace to receive his Knighthood.

Sir Tom and his wife Lady Elsie after he received his Knighthood.

*'It was a great occasion for me and my wife to go down to Buckingham Palace. I went on to get the OBE, CBE and Knighthood and it was presented by Her Majesty the Queen, and I was absolutely thrilled about that.'*

Sir Tom Finney

Sir Tom, Lady Elsie, Barbara and Brian outside Buckingham Palace before he received his Knighthood on 17 February 1998.

Sir Tom and Lady Elsie celebrating their golden wedding anniversary in 1995.

Sir Tom and Lady Elsie viewing the National Football Museum at Deepdale, Preston, in 2001 of which he is now the President.

Sir Tom pulls on a special shirt to mark his 80th birthday in front of the stand bearing his name at Deepdale.

Sir Tom celebrates his 85th birthday at Ingol Golf Club.

Sir Tom Finney during his book signing session at the W H Smith store in Chorley in 2003.

# CHAPTER TWO
# *Playing Days*

*'Tom Finney was a fantastic player. You will never see his like today. In his prime it was almost impossible to take the ball from him. Now there would be all sorts of plans to stop him. That is how big he was. But Tom also helps with charity events and in his own part of the world in Preston, he is a god, an absolute god and rightly so.*

*Wherever you go in the world and especially if you mention Preston North End, people say Tommy Finney. He has been, and still is, a great source of pride for the people of Preston.'*

England teammate Sir Bobby Charlton

*'I will always remember my playing career with fond memories, and though there may be the odd regret the main feeling is one of immense pride.'*

Sir Tom Finney

*'Tom was crafty, quick and elusive. He could beat you on either side without breaking stride. When he had the ball, that was it, you'd never get it back. A brilliant, exceptional player.'*

Preston North End teammate Bill Shankly

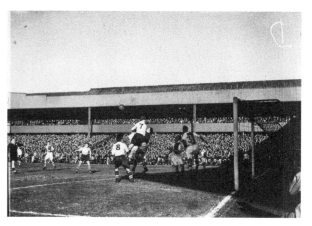

Preston North End and England Footballer of the Year 1954, Tom Finney shows one of his many international caps to the Northern Rhodesia Sportsman of the Year 1953, Inspector Wapamesa of the North Rhodesian Police, after giving a coaching exhibition in Lusaka.

'Ask any footballer who has been chosen to represent the land of his birth, and he will tell you that no feeling quite compares.'

Sir Tom Finney

'*I won the Player of the Year twice in '54 and '57, which was a great achievement in those days and I was very thrilled.*'

Sir Tom Finney

Preston North End mascot Bob Roe leads the team out in the mid-1950s.

*'Good players always want to play for the best clubs and there are some, like me, who only want to play for one club. I was a bit of a rarity back then too.'*

Sir Tom Finney

A famous photograph of Sir Tom from the Easter Monday game against Blackburn Rovers at Deepdale on 10 April 1950. This image became known as The Magnet as Sir Tom draws attention from Rovers' Eckersley, Horton and Holt.

*'After travelling the world representing my country for 12 years, I could only offer my grateful thanks to those who made it possible. I would willingly have paid the FA to play.'*
Sir Tom Finney

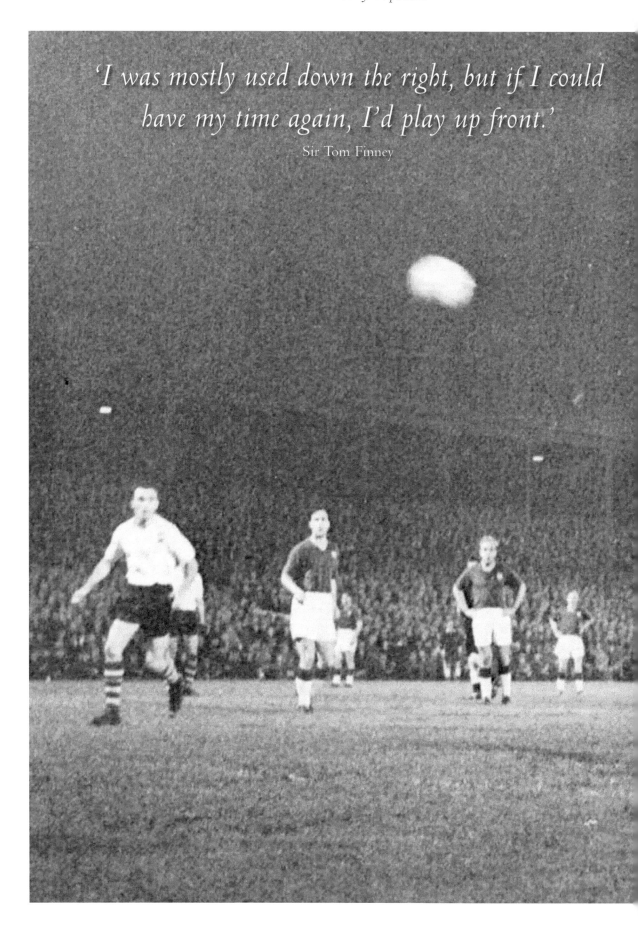

'I was mostly used down the right, but if I could have my time again, I'd play up front.'

Sir Tom Finney

'It was just a number as far as I was concerned. I don't think it would have made a difference what number I wore. I just happened to be playing on the outside-right and I also played as number-9 and number-11 as well during my time at North End.'

Sir Tom Finney on the famous number-seven jersey

# CHAPTER THREE
# *Life at Preston North End*

*'There was nothing that Tom couldn't do on a football field. He could head a ball with the strength of a lion, score goals with either foot, and in a one-on-one with Tom you could pack up and go home.'*

Preston North End teammate Les Dagger

*'I was born and bred in Preston and always wanted to play for Preston North End. I think people here were proud I never moved away. That's why they have stuck with me over the years!'*

Sir Tom Finney

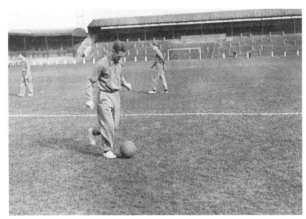

*'Tom's skill was quite remarkable. Much of it was due to the fact he had fast muscles like Matthews. They could both stop and start more quickly than his opponents'.'*

England manager Sir Walter Winterbottom

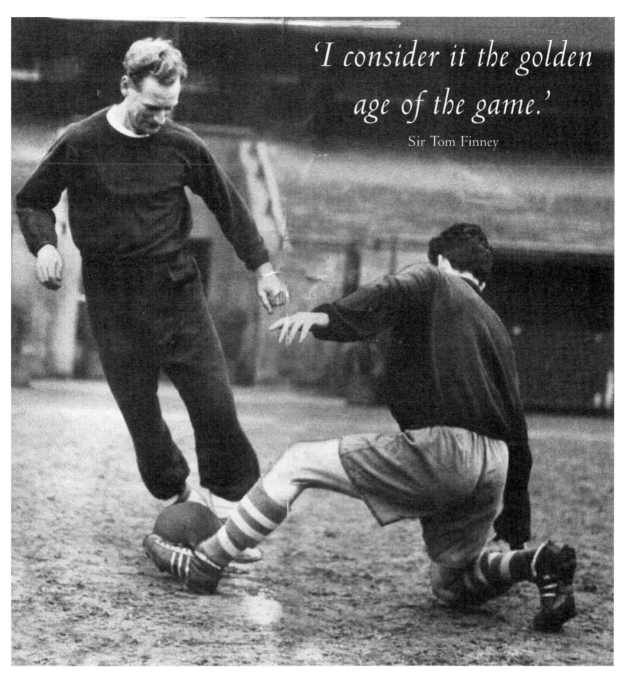

*'I consider it the golden age of the game.'*

Sir Tom Finney

The Tarleton Juniors football team of 1952–53 lined up for this picture at a presentation dance in Tarleton Conservative Hall, at which Tom Finney was guest of honour.

Preston's most famous son signing autographs at Ribbleton Methodist Church Christmas fair back in 1951. The cub scout with him is Stephen Brooks

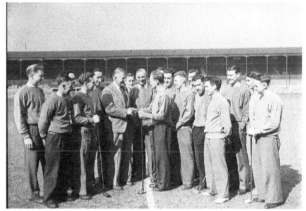

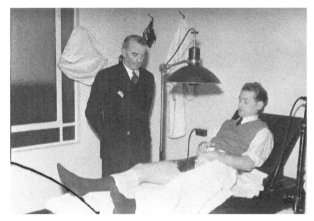

Tom Finney with future England winger Peter Thompson.

*'I feel we played in better times and it was a sport first and foremost, not a business as it has become today'*

Sir Tom Finney

Tom Finney shakes hands with Jimmy Milne, watched by Willie Cunningham (left) and other members of the Preston North End staff.

Tom Finney with Peter Thompson at Fishwick Hall Golf Club in 1960.

On tour with England in Portugal on the steps of the hotel. Front row, left to right, Wilf Mannion, Jackie Milburn, Tom Finney, Billy Wright and Stanley Mortensen.

Tom Finney with Nat Lofthouse and Dennis Violet at a presentation evening at Earlstown Town Hall shortly after his retirement in 1960.

Tom Finney as player-manager of the Football Association touring team in 1961.

Tom Finney was on hand to present the Sunday League champions' and Riding Cup winners' trophies to Leyland St Ambrose footballers in 1954–55, which prompted Bill Tattersall of Clayton-le-Woods to reflect, 'What an honour it was to receive them from the greatest footballer on the planet.' Bill is second from the left on the front row.

Over £150 was raised for Kirkham parish church at this garden party in the grounds of Kirkham Grammar School. Pictured are the vicar, the Rev A.M.P Wilson, Tom Finney with his daughter, Barbara, and Mr D. Norwood, the school's headmaster.

# CHAPTER FOUR
# *The 1954 FA Cup Final*

*'It was a disappointing game from Preston's point of view and particularly from my own point of view. It was fair to say I had one of my poorest games for North End when really what I wanted was the game of my life.'*

Sir Tom Finney

The team pose in their Wembley suits.

Sir Tom checks out the official team outfits for their big day.

The proudest moment of Sir Tom Finney's Preston North End career came on 1 May 1954 when he led his team out at Wembley for the FA Cup Final. In a hard-fought match the team were beaten 3–2 by West Bromwich Albion in front of 100,000 fans.

The line-up for the 1954 FA Cup Final, headed by club captain Sir Tom.

Sir Tom introduces his teammates to special guest the Queen Mother.

The dejected Preston North End team leave the pitch after the defeat.

Preston North End players drown their sorrows at the post-match dinner at the Savoy Hotel, London.

Tens of thousands of people took to the streets of Preston to welcome their heroes back from Wembley.

Sir Tom raises Preston North End mascot Bob Roe to wave to the crowd gathered on Preston's Flag Market to welcome the players home.

# CHAPTER FIVE

# *The Final Match*

*'Tom was the best ever. Bestie maybe was close to him, but he was a better player than Matthews. He could play equally as well at outside-right or outside-left.*

*'He was different class - you couldn't buy him today. You'd have to rob Fort Knox to pay for him if he was playing now. He was a great player end of story. And a gentleman too, which is more important. I can't speak too highly of him as a person.'*

Preston North End teammate Tommy Docherty

Sir Tom's last game for Preston North End was a League match against Luton Town at Deepdale on 30 April 1960. His 473rd appearance for North End saw a 2–0 victory in front of 30,000 fans – double the normal attendance at the time. Sir Tom checks his fan mail ahead of his last appearance for Preston North End.

Passers-by looking at the Tom Finney Testimonial Fund display in the window of the *Lancashire Evening Post* office in Friargate.

Sir Tom meets the press in the countdown to his last appearance for Preston North End.

Players from both sides link hands to sing *Auld Lang Syne* and *For He's a Jolly Good Fellow.*

*'I went on to play until I was 38 years of age, which I thought in those days was looked upon as a pretty special occasion.'*

Sir Tom Finney

'There is a tendency to look back and exaggerate. People say the older you are the better player you were. But in Tom's case, if you speak to anyone who played in that era, they will say that Tom Finney was a truly great player.'

Former Liverpool captain Alan Hansen

Sir Tom stands on a table to address the fans after the game, telling them, 'It's such a sad, sad day for me but today is a day I will remember forever and thank you all for making it so grand.'

*'Sir Tom made me the player I was and I had many an England game with him. He is a really nice guy. He had loyalty to spare. He was loyal to his family, loyal to Preston North End and loyal to the England football team.'*

England teammate Nat Lofthouse

Sir Tom walks out of Deepdale's players' entrance for the last time as a Preston North End footballer.

Sir Tom takes off his boots for the last time after the Luton Town match in April 1960.

CHAPTER SIX

# Love Affair with the Game

*'I'd heard about this Finney fella when I was a lad in Scotland, but the first time I saw him play I couldn't believe it. He was a wizard, and it was like he was wearing magic boots. He had such incredible guile and skill. His speed of thought and his anticipation was breathtaking. Every era has a great player, but "our Tommy" was the greatest of them all. Nobody will ever convince me otherwise.'*

Preston North End teammate Sammy Taylor

Sir Tom helps remove the turf when the Deepdale grass was replaced by a plastic pitch for a few seasons.

Sir Tom on the Kop at Deepdale before its demolition in 1997.

Guest of honour at Wembley for the 1996 Charity Shield, Sir Tom presents the trophy to victorious captain Roy Keane.

Sir Tom walks along the red carpet at the start of an FA Cup match between Stockport County and Preston North End in 1998 to celebrate receiving his knighthood.

Sir Tom discusses the game with former Preston North End manager Gary Peters.

David Lucas receives his England Under-20 cap from Sir Tom at Deepdale in 1997.

Sir Tom with his 83rd birthday cake during the presentation at half-time in the Preston North End versus Brighton & Hove Albion Coca-Cola Championship match at Deepdale, Preston.

Sir Tom at the new Wembley.

Sir Tom joins Preston North End manager Billy Davies on the pitch before the Championship Play-off Final at Cardiff's Millennium Stadium in 2005.

Kirkham & Wesham FC's civic presentation after winning the 2008 FA Vase with, left to right, Sir Tom Finney, Martin Booken from the PFA, team captain Dougie Shaw and Councillor Alan Whittaker, chairman of Lancashire County Council.

Sir Tom discusses the game with Preston North End player Chris Neale in 2008.

Sir Tom casts an eye over his autobiography on the plastic pitch at Deepdale.

'*People talk about the present-day awards and I think I was rewarded by the club which went on to name a stand after me, which I feel very, very proud of and is a great achievement when I think about other players.*'

Sir Tom Finney

# CHAPTER SEVEN

# Life after Football

'Tom Finney was the greatest-ever footballer, better than Pele, George Best or Maradona. But Finney was not only the greatest player ever to grace a football field, he was a decent human being, a fine gentleman and the greatest ambassador Preston North End could have.'

Preston North End teammate John Barton

Bob Batey, Kendal's Preston North End supporters' club president, hands over a suitcase to Sir Tom as a retirement gift in 1961.

Sir Tom receives the book of signatures of those who subscribed to his fund from Alderman Mrs F. Hoskin in December 1960.

Sir Tom has a game of bagatelle with members of Star Youth Club after opening the new clubroom in Brook Street, Preston, in 1962.

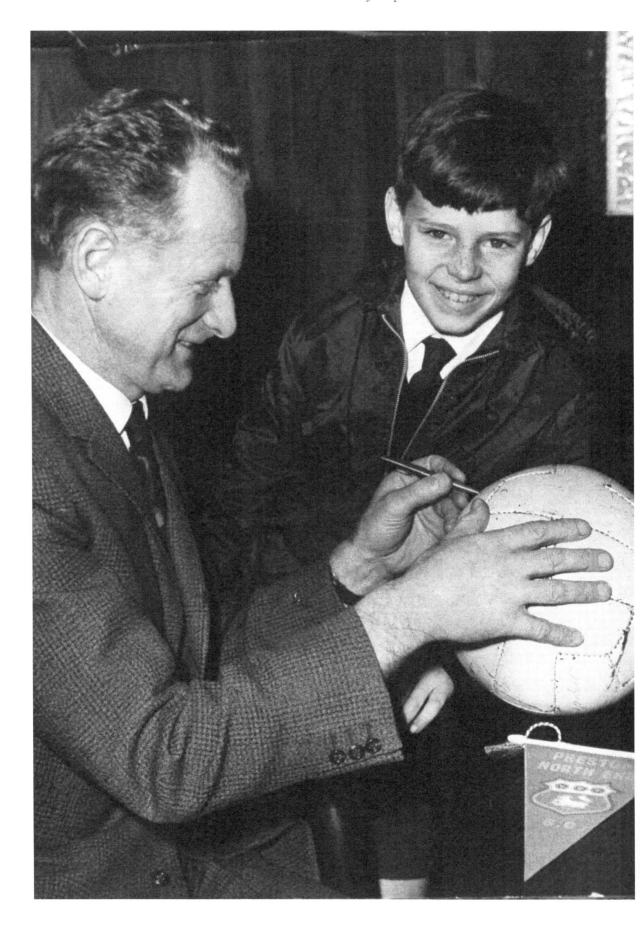

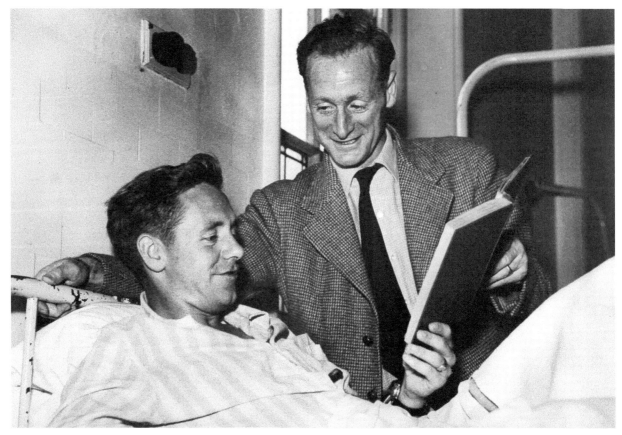

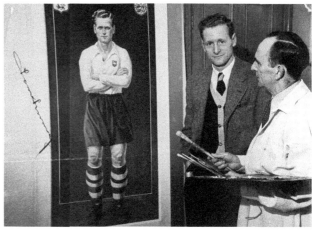

'I had about half a dozen sittings. It was pretty much unheard of to paint a footballer in those days and there was a bit of leg-pulling in the dressing room. I used to come to the Harris Gallery on school trips, but I never thought my picture would end up here. It is not just an honour for me, it is for Preston North End and football in general.'

Sir Tom Finney

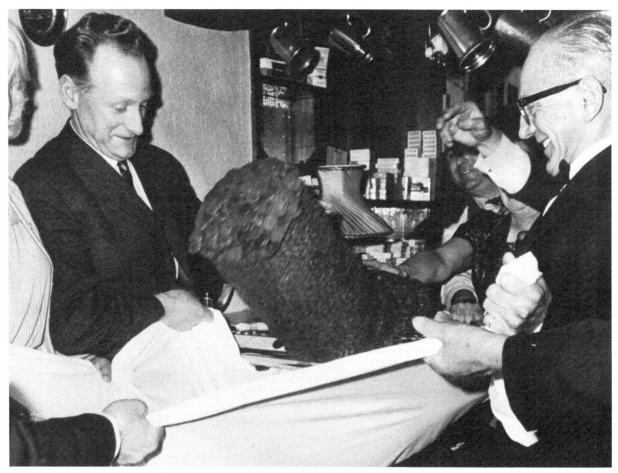

Sir Tom topples a pile of pennies at the Golden Ball pub in Longton, in aid of Preston and District Mentally Handicapped Children's Society in 1965.

Sir Tom toasts the opening of the Tom Finney pub in Penwortham in 1975.

Sir Tom presents at the Odeon Cinema in Preston in 1976.

Former German prisoner of war Werner Gerlach meets Sir Tom in 1977. Herr Gerlach was held at a camp near Samlesbury, Lancashire, during World War Two.

Sir Tom receives the Freedom of Preston from city councillors at a special ceremony in the town hall in 1979.

Sir Tom smashes open a bottle of pennies at the Brookfield Arms, Preston, watched by Miss Matthew Brown in aid of the Sunshine Bus in 1981.

The Anchor Inn at Hutton re-opens in 1984 with a little help from Sir Tom.

From 1984 to 1987 Sir Tom served as chairman of Preston Health Authority. Here he is pictured outside of the Royal Preston Hospital.

Sir Tom joins *Lancashire Evening Post* readers on a flight on board Concorde to celebrate the newspaper's 100th birthday in 1986.

Sir Tom at Preston Parish Church in 1986.

Sir Tom receives an honorary degree from Preston Polytechnic in 1988.

Getting to grips with Stan Levi Walch in 1993 to celebrate the local boxer's birthday and help raise £3,000 for Christies.

Club president Sir Tom leads the bowling at Ashton Park Bowling Club in 1995 on President's Day.

Sir Tom returns to his old school Deepdale Modern Junior School for a kickabout in the yard.

Fans young and old vie for an autograph in 1996.

At the opening of the Preston North End shop on Preston's Flag Market in 1997.

Sir Tom with senior partner Peter Scholes (left) and Peter Turner at the new Forbes Dolphin offices in Preston in 1998.

Sir Tom officially opens the Greenbank Building at the University of Central Lancashire in 1998.

Enjoying a pint after opening the Phantom Winger pub, named in his honour, in Fulwood, Preston, in 1998.

At the Night of Knights Tribute to Sir Tom Finney at Preston North End, with his wife Lady Elsie, left, and Lady Charlton in 1998.

Sir Tom is a long-time patron of the Baby Beat Appeal to raise money for premature babies in Preston.

Jean Gough, Sir Stanley Matthews' daughter, her grandson, four-year-old Cameron Gough, and Sir Tom at the ceremony to unveil a plaque at the home where Sir Stanley Matthews was born in Stoke.

Alex Swales(4) gets a little help from Sir Tom in the new classroom at Ribbleton Avenue Infant School, Preston, in 2001.

Getting behind Comic Relief for Red Nose Day in 2003.

Sir Tom supports the Sainsbury's Exercise Bike Marathon at the Deepdale store for BBC Children In Need in 2004.

Sir Tom opens the Holme Slack Sports Zone in 2004.

Sir Tom with his Lifetime Achievement Award at the Preston City Charter Awards ceremony at Preston's Guild Hall in 2004.

Sir Tom kicks the first ball at the opening of the Moor Park football pitches in 2005, as pupils from Deepdale Junior School and Moor Park High School cheer him on.

Sir Tom is awarded the Lifetime Contribution to Sport Award at the 2006 Preston Sports Awards.

Young fan William Roe gets his shirt signed by Sir Tom at Preston North End's 1950s celebration day.

Sir Tom opens a new resource centre at Preston College. Here he is pictured with the college's five-a-side football team, who were national champions in 2007.

Richard Rayton has a suprise meeting in 2007 with his fooballing hero during a tour of the National Football Museum at Deepdale. The 99-year-old used to cycle from Freckleton to watch Sir Tom play at Deepdale.

Sir Tom met and offered words of advice to the new trainees at Preston North End in 2007. From left to right, Dominic Collins, Jack Cudworth, Nathan Fairhurst and Danny Mayor.

Sir Tom joins former England and Preston North End colleague Tommy Thompson on the first tee at the Sir Tom Finney Golf Classic held at Ashton and Lea Golf Club in 2007.

Meeting members of the Kings Royal Hussars on Preston's Flag Market in 2008.

Opening the play area at Moorfield School, Preston, in 2008.

Sir Tom returns to Italy where he served as a tank driver and mechanic with the Eighth Army during World War Two and visits the Coriano ridge war cemetery near Rimini.

Sir Tom with Les Halliwell and Roy Boyles at a reunion of soldiers who served in the Trieste area of Italy from 1945 to 1954.

# CHAPTER EIGHT

# Star among Stars

'No better player than Tom has ever won an England shirt. He was the best in the world - a genius.'

England captain and teammate Billy Wright

'Sir Tom was a marvellous player and he is a perfect gentleman as well.'

England captain Bryan Robson

England greats Geoff Hurst, Sir Tom, Bobby Moore, Johnny Haynes, Stan Mortensen and Alan Mullery during a recording of *A Question of Sport* in 1970.

Sir Tom welcomes the Queen Mother at St Oswald's Youth Club, Preston.

Fellow England winger Peter Barnes and Sir Tom chat about the game at a meeting of the Preston North End Supporters' Club in 1977.

Sir Tom and Sir Bobby Charlton celebrate the opening of the Tom Finney Pub.

Sir Tom with glamour model Gillian Duxbury.

Lancashire comedy legend Les Dawson fools around ahead of a golf challenge with Sir Tom.

One time Preston North End manager Jimmy Milne, Sir Tom and footballer turned television pundit Jimmy Hill.

Blackpool star Stan Mortensen, Sir Tom and Liverpool striker Ian St John.

Sir Tom with former Manchester City manager Joe Mercer and former Manchester United manager Matt Busby.

Former Preston North End teammates Tommy Docherty, Sir Tom and Willie Cunningham.

Sir Tom and Nat Lofthouse in 1989 at an exhibition celebrating the Bolton Wanderers star.

Footballing knights Sir Tom and Sir Stanley Matthews pictured in 1990 at Old Trafford at the launch of 'Art of Sport', which pays tribute to former giants of the game.

Manchester United star Denis Law, Sir Tom and Bolton Wanderers favourite Nat Lofthouse with Sports Minister Colin Moynihan in 1990.

Sir Tom Finney and fellow Preston North End great Tommy Thompson at the ex-Preston North End Heroes signing session at the National Football Museum.

Sir Tom and HRH Prince Charles during a Royal visit to Preston North End in 1997.

*'It was the first time I had met Prince Charles, although I had previously met the Queen when I went to Buckingham Palace to be knighted.'*

Sir Tom Finney

*'I had a game of table football with him which was just a bit of fun. We didn't really get much chance to talk a lot but he did say he was impressed with the ground.'*

Sir Tom Finney

*'It was a very enjoyable day and Prince Charles seemed a very nice, pleasant fellow who was easy to get on with.'*

Sir Tom Finney

Sir Tom and Sir Bobby Charlton with a pair of Sir Tom's boots from the National Football Museum in 1997.

'*Bobby Charlton was an up-and-coming star when I was finishing. He so impressed me. After seeing him for the first time, I knew he had the makings of an outstanding player. His ability stood out. When he came in the England side, he was very, very quiet. He listened and learned.*'

Sir Tom Finney

Football meets rugby: Sir Tom and England World Cup-winning rugby star Jason Robinson in 1997.

Eastenders star Tom Watt joins Sir Tom Finney on the Preston North End pitch in 1998.

Sir Tom with footballer Mark Hughes after receiving his Knighthood from the Queen at Buckingham Palace in 1998.

Sir Bobby Charlton, Sir Tom Finney and Nat Lofthouse at the Night of Knights Tribute to Sir Tom Finney at Preston North End in 1998.

*'I was a lucky lad, I had Matthews on my right wing and Finney on my left and that's what made me an international footballer and goalscorer.'*

Nat Lofthouse

Sir Tom and England teammate Nat Lofthouse leave their feet impressions so they can be cast in stone for the Walk of Fame at Preston North End in 2000.

Sir Tom Finney and Nat Lofthouse share a joke at the launch of the Hall of Fame at the National Football Museum in 2002.

Sepp Blatter, President of FIFA, meets Sir Tom Finney during his visit to open the FIFA Centenary Exhibition at the National Football Museum in 2004.

*'In an age when football needs role models of fine character, honesty and modesty, the image of Tom Finney is more valuable and more valid then ever.'*
Sepp Blatter, FIFA General Secretary

Spurs legend Dave Mackay, Sir Tom Finney, Manchester United manager Sir Alex Ferguson and former Crewe Alexandra manager Dario Gradi at the National Football Museum's Hall of Fame inauguration in 2004.

*'The people of Preston are right to be proud of Sir Tom. I remember growing up and seeing him play. He was a real footballer. Two great feet, great balance, oh just fantastic. Him and Stanley Matthews were something else.'*

Sir Alex Ferguson

Sir Bobby Robson, Jimmy Armfield and Sir Tom Finney at Jimmy Armfield's charity dinner at the Paradise Room at Blackpool Pleasure Beach in 2004.

*'I honestly believe he was one of the greatest, if not the greatest, player in the world. With Tom it is not just about the football because he is also a great man who has never changed.'*

Jimmy Armfield

Boxing champion Michael Jennings, Sir Tom and comedian Dave Spikey at the 2005 Red Rose awards at Park Hall Hotel, Charnock Richard.

Former Manchester City goalkeeper Bert Trautmann with Sir Tom Finney during his visit to the National Football Museum in 2005.

England cricketer and fellow Prestonian Andrew Flintoff joins Sir Tom at a charity evening in the cricketer's name at Preston Grasshoppers Rugby Club in 2005.

*'He is a very ordinary, down to earth lad and I have always found him very pleasant anytime we have bumped into each other over the years. I watched the Ashes series and there is no doubt Andrew was one of the principal reasons we won.'*

Sir Tom Finney

Ivor Broadis (Newcastle and England player), Sammy Taylor (Preston North End and Scotland player), Sir Tom Finney, Bobby Smith (Tottenham Hotspur and England), Tommy Thompson (Preston North End and England) and Tommy Docherty (Preston North End and Scotland) at a charity auction in 2006.

Governor of the Bank of England Mervyn King chats with Sir Tom at The National Football Museum as they check out the old FA Cup in 2006.

Sir Tom and fellow Prestonian Mark Lawrenson admiring a Stagecoach Preston North End bus in livery celebrating the club's history in 2007.

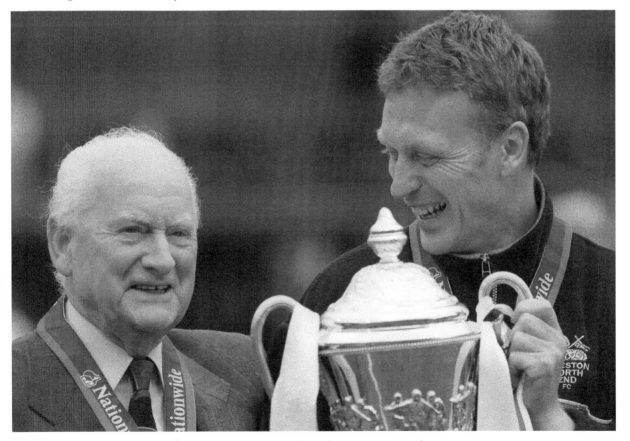

Sir Tom shares a joke with former Preston North End manager David Moyes.

Sir Tom receives his Lifetime Achievement Award for Contribution to Sport from Steve Rider at the 2007 Variety Sports Awards Dinner.

Sir Tom is joined by rugby great Billy Boston and Chelsea star Ron 'Chopper' Harris at the Preston North End Players' annual in the Great Room at Deepdale in 2008.

Preston North End players Sean St Ledger and Neil Mellor with Sir Tom in 2008.

Sir Tom with comic Frank Carson at A Big Knight Out in honour of Sir Tom at the Preston Guild Hall in 2008.

With Coronation Street barmaid Katherine Kelly, alias Becky Granger, at the launch of his Big Knight Out charity show at the Mall, Preston, in 2008.

Football greats Wilf Mannion, Sir Stanley Matthews, Nat Lofthouse, Tommy Lawton, George Hardwick and Sir Tom line up for the ultimate fantasy football team.

*"Stan was such an outstanding player. He was the greatest in my era in terms of close control. In those days you weren't expected to go back and tackle and his game was attacking the full-back. I can recall on so many occasions him having great games for England. I'm sure Stan could have played in the modern game. The game's all about skill and he had it in abundance. It's like asking if Maradona or Pele could have played today but you know the answer because they had stacks of ability."*

Sir Tom Finney

# CHAPTER NINE

# A Lasting Memorial

*'Tom Finney was a magician. A footballer in the master class. He was a complete one off and one of the greatest players the world has ever seen.'*

Preston North End teammate Tommy Thompson

*'His skill was quite exceptional.'*

England teammate Johnny Haynes

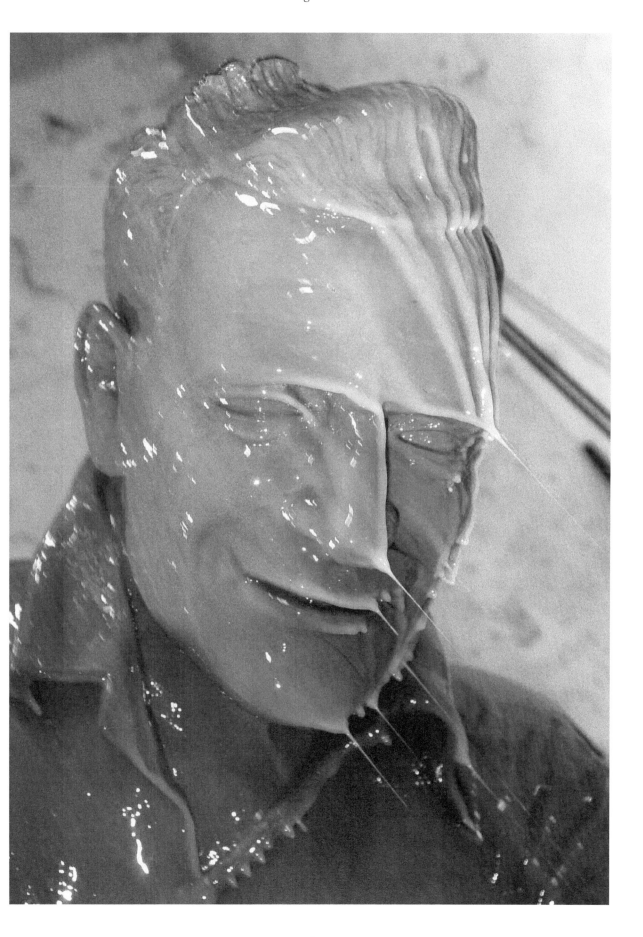

The famous splash photograph was taken on 25 August 1956 during a match between Preston North End and Chelsea on the London club's Stamford Bridge pitch. The wing wizard was captured shielding the ball from Chelsea's Walter Bellett in a dramatic arc of water during a game which was deluged by a torrential downpour.

Sir Tom remembers, 'Nowadays, they wouldn't have started the game, it had rained so hard. There was a downpour during the game and I was going through a pool of water to get the ball. It was a fantastic photograph. The cameraman must have had his lens perfectly set, you can even see the individual drops of water.'

*'I really treasure the fact that the club decided they would make a statue of the splash and that's at Deepdale and is seen by many, many people.'*

Sir Tom Finney

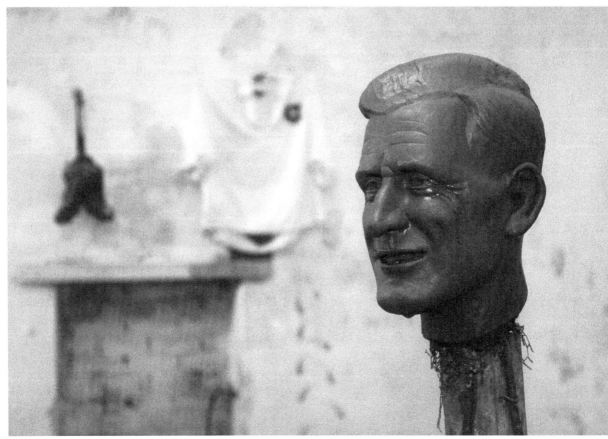

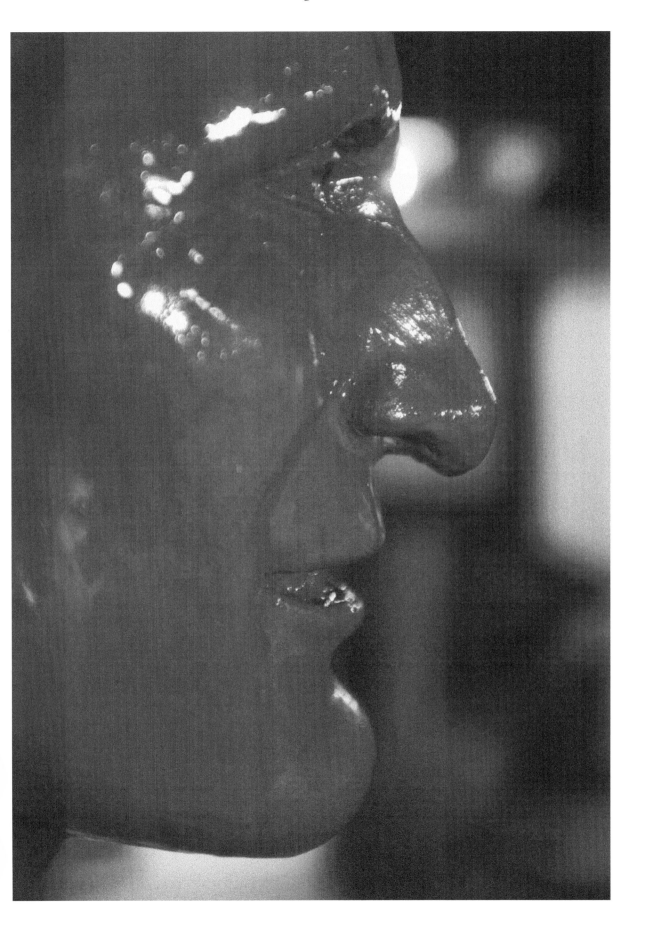

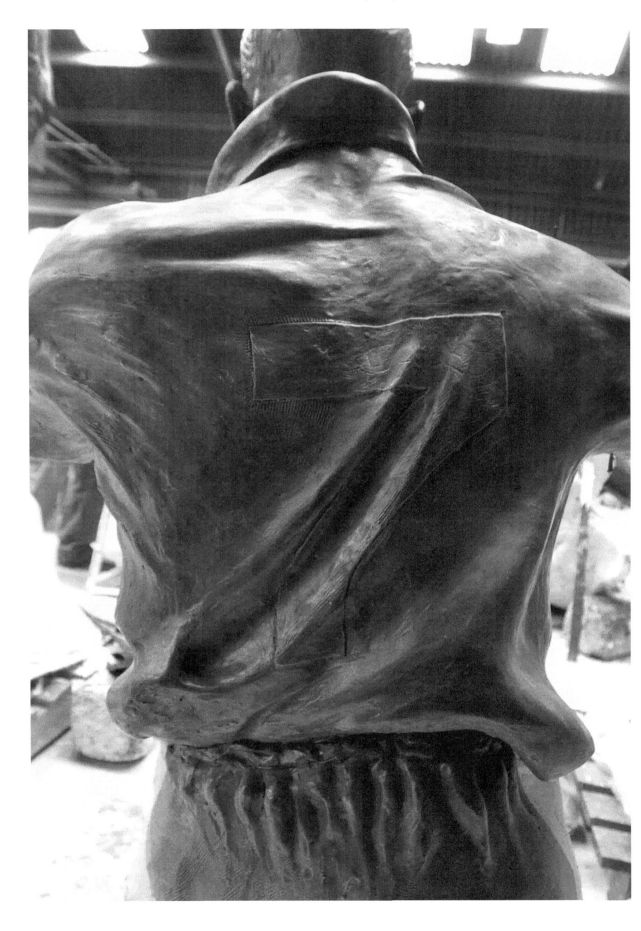

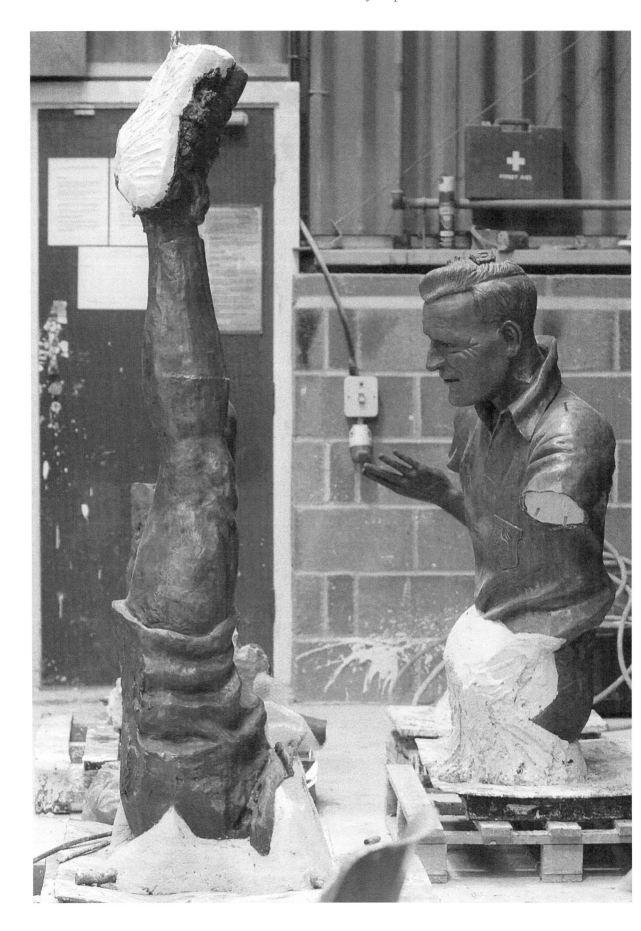

Sir Tom unveils the £200,000 splash statue outside Deepdale on 31 July 2004.

Tommy Docherty shines Sir Tom's boots as the former teammates share a joke.

'It's a great honour. It's more than 40 years since I stopped playing and now to have this beautiful statue. It's been marvellous for me and I'm very proud to be a Prestonian.'

Sir Tom Finney

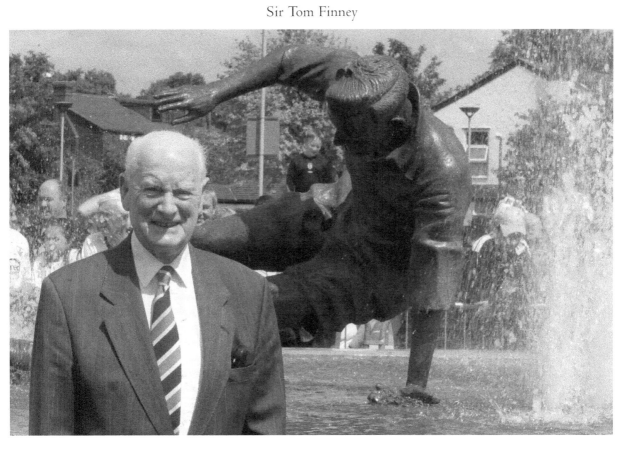

'By heck, he could play.'

England footballer Joe Mercer